About Demos

Demos is a greenhouse for new ideas which can improve the quality of our lives. As an independent think tank, we aim to create an open resource of knowledge and learning that operates beyond traditional party politics.

We connect researchers, thinkers and practitioners to an international network of people changing politics. Our ideas regularly influence government policy, but we also work with companies, NGOs, colleges and professional bodies.

Demos knowledge is organised around five themes, which combine to create new perspectives. The themes are democracy, learning, enterprise, quality of life and global change.

But we also understand that thinking by itself is not enough. Demos has helped to initiate a number of practical projects which are delivering real social benefit through the redesign of public services.

We bring together people from a wide range of backgrounds to cross-fertilise ideas and experience. By working with Demos, our partners develop a sharper insight into the way ideas shape society. For Demos, the process is as important as the final product.

www.demos.co.uk

First published in 2004
© Demos
Some rights reserved – see copyright licence for details

ISBN 1 84180 127 5
Typeset by Land & Unwin, Bugbrooke
Designed by R&D&Co
Printed by PrintFlow, London

For further information and
subscription details please contact:

Demos
The Mezzanine
Elizabeth House
39 York Road
London SE1 7NQ

telephone: 020 7401 5330
email: hello@demos.co.uk
web: www.demos.co.uk

The Risk Management of Everything

Rethinking the politics of uncertainty

Michael Power

DEM⊙S

Contents

Acknowledgements

This essay began life as an inaugural professorial lecture, 'The new risk management', given at the London School of Economics in December 1999. The author thanks the Trustees of the Institute of Chartered Accountants in England and Wales, and the Economic and Social Research Council for financial support. The author is also grateful for helpful comments from Tom Bentley, Julia Black, Rachel Briggs, Robert Bruce, Bill Durodie, Martin Evans, Bridget Hutter, Jimi Irwin, Sue Mayer, Caroline Muller, Nick Pidgeon, Henry Rothstein, Andy Stirling, James Strachan, Christopher Swinson, James Wilsdon and Brian Wynne. Particular thanks are due to Paul Skidmore and Eddie Gibb of Demos and to Julie Pickard.

Michael Power
June 2004

Michael Power is P.D. Leake Professor of Accounting and a Director of the ESRC Centre for the Analysis of Risk and Regulation (CARR) at the London School of Economics, where he has worked since 1987. He is a fellow of the Institute of Chartered Accountants in England and Wales (ICAEW) and an associate member of the UK Chartered Institute of Taxation. He has held visiting fellowships at the Institute for Advanced Study, Berlin and All Souls College, Oxford. Research interests focus mainly on the changing relationship between financial accounting, auditing and risk management. He is author of *The Audit Explosion* (Demos, 1994) and *The Audit Society: Rituals of Verification* (Oxford University Press, 1999), which has been translated into Italian and Japanese, and is currently being translated into French.

1. Introduction

the risk management explosion

Can we know the risks we face, now or in the future? No, we cannot: but yes, we must act as if we do.[1]

Risk management and risk 'talk' are all around us. The risk-based description of organisational life is conspicuous. Not only private sector companies, but hospitals, schools, universities and many other public organisations, including the very highest levels of central government, have all been invaded to varying degrees by ideas about risk and its management.

○   Why has this happened and what are its consequences?
○   Is this just one more management craze with questionable benefits and potentially adverse effects?
○   Or is it a rational response to an increasingly risky world?
○   Is the growing organisational preoccupation with risk management a symptom of failing control in a complex environment, or is it a basis for refocusing entrepreneurial energy?
○   Governments and large organisations must always act as if they are in control, so is risk management simply the new game of reassurance, an audit explosion in new clothes, or a basis for innovation and change?

And what of the general public and its relationship to this ubiquitous risk management? Does it enhance public confidence in private and public sector organisations, or is it simply a managerial smokescreen, deflecting attention from the more fundamental fact that individuals are increasingly alone with risk, unable to trust the very institutions designed to absorb it on their behalf?

These questions motivate an analysis of the 'risk management of everything', a motif for one of the major public policy challenges of the early twenty-first century.

Risk talk and risk management practices

Risk talk and risk management practices, rather like auditing in the 1990s, embody the fundamentally contradictory nature of organisational and political life. On the one hand, there is a functional and political need to maintain myths of control and manageability, because this is what various interested constituencies and stakeholders seem to demand. Risks must be made auditable and governable. On the other hand, there is a consistent stream of failures, scandals and disasters which challenge and threaten organisations, suggesting a world which is out of control and where failure may be endemic, and in which the organisational interdependencies are so intricate that no single locus of control has a grasp of them.

Risk management organises what cannot be organised, because individuals, corporations and governments have little choice but to do so. The risk management of everything holds out the promise of manageability in new areas. But it also implies a new way of allocating responsibility for decisions which must be made in potentially undecidable situations.

Who bears the risk?

Many agencies in society which have traditionally played the role of taking risk on behalf of the public, such as insurance companies, financial services organisations and financial professionals, seem in fact to be handing risks back as part of their own risk management. Indeed, the risk management of everything is characterised by the growth of risk management strategies that displace valuable – but vulnerable – professional judgement in favour of defendable process. The state's orientation to risk has also been transformed. The UK government has recently become only too aware of big system and project failures, and the vulnerabilities they create. In the fields of energy provision, public transport, health, financial services and large-scale infrastructure there have been major public crises. Following the BSE crisis, and failures in school examinations and passport applications systems, risk management ideas have moved to the heart of government itself. Risk management is now at the centre stage of public service delivery and is a model of organisation in its own right.

Notwithstanding these efforts, faith in the role of the state as absorber, collectiviser and redistributor of risk may be in decline. Government is suspected of substituting risk management for political argument.

The rise of risk management

Risk management is much more than a technical analytical practice; it also embodies significant values and ideals, not least of accountability and responsibility. Historically, a public politics of risk management, particularly in the field of health, has been concerned with the transparency and accountability of scientific expertise in decisions about risk acceptance. Since the mid-1990s, risk management and private corporate governance agendas have become intertwined, if not identical. Since 1995 (the year of the collapse of Barings bank and of the Brent Spar crisis for Shell), being a 'good' organisation has become synonymous with having a broad and formal risk management programme. Risk analysis, the traditional technical home territory of risk management, has been subsumed within a larger accountability and control framework.[2]

An expanding knowledge base for risk management

Evidence for this transformation in the meaning and scope of risk and its management is to be found in a policy, business and regulatory literature explosion since the mid-1990s, providing a knowledge base from which corporations and government can draw.[3] In the UK, slender guidance documents such as the 'Turnbull Report' have become powerful points of reference in a reform process which has seen the emergence of standardised organisational forms, such as risk committees, appearing throughout the private and public sectors.[4] A casual internet search using the term 'risk management' yields numerous professional articles in areas as diverse as anaesthetics and charities, and all seem to adopt a similar framework.

Multiple textbooks and articles on 'enterprise' and 'integrated' risk management have been published since the late 1990s, a period which has seen the flowering of many new practitioner magazines with the word 'risk' in their titles, and the conscious amendment of extant titles to include the word risk.[5] Existing occupational associations, particularly those with strong foundations in insurance, a traditional stronghold of risk management thinking, have also taken up a generic risk management agenda and their websites have become reference points for new risk management thinking which is rapidly diffused.[6]

This explosion of risk management ideas and blueprints is a collection of aspirations and ideas, a rhetoric which may be well ahead of practice. Unlike the expansion of auditing in the 1980s, states and politicians do not appear to have been major direct pressures for change, although they are adopters of risk management thinking. New models of organisation and regulation are emerging from various private sector sources, and consultants and professional service firms are conspicuously the creators of new templates for managing risk, sensing opportunities for using risk to redefine their strategic significance and value.[7]

The risk management of everything
Origins
This phenomenal expansion of the risk industry reflects a number of different but convergent pressures for change in organisational practices for dealing with *uncertainty*. There has been a fusion of

ideas about organisational governance and corporate responsibility. New models of regulation are in vogue, and there have been changes in attitude to the traditional mechanics of risk transfer with a greater accent on risk communication. In addition, technological changes in information systems have created new risk management possibilities. Scandals and crises of the past ten years have also been catalysts for the emergence of a conception of risk management with wide scope, unifying traditionally separate areas, such as health and safety, insurance and project management in a single model, but also absorbing new objects of concern.[8] Even concepts of national security and ideas of 'preventative' military action are being thought of within the conceptual architecture of risk management.

Risk has entered private and public sector management thinking to become an *organising concept* as never before.[9] Since the mid-1990s considerable effort has been expended on making risk management into a value proposition and in both private and public sectors the concept of risk is being enrolled in a new focus on *outcomes* and *performance*. In the private sector this is visible in efforts to link investments in control activities to organisational objectives and value creation within frameworks for enterprise-wide risk management (ERM). In the public sector 'risk', rather like customer responsiveness, is emerging as the basis for self-challenging management practices in the absence of direct competitive pressures.

However, while these rhetorics of value, integration and innovation may be upbeat, it will be argued that these aspirations must overcome the overwhelming tendency for the new risk management to exacerbate *process*. In both the public and private sectors, risk management is part of a new style of organisational discipline and accountability. Herein lies one of the major risks of the risk management of everything.

What is risk?

The risk management of everything is intended to suggest that more and more events and things are being seen and described in terms of 'risk', even though the concept remains elusive, contested and 'inherently controversial'.[10] Various specialist definitions and classifications exist in the attempt to secure its meaning, and these definitions reflect specific institutional interests. In some traditions (health and safety), risk is equated with hazards and dangers; for others (finance) it is a matter of volatility in expected outcomes, both negative and positive. However, the very vagueness and ambiguity of 'risk', a fact which troubles expert commentators, is in fact a necessary feature of its widespread impact. From this point of view, the question 'what is risk?' is less important than the question: 'how do we know risk and what are the social and economic institutions which embody that knowledge?'.[11]

It has been famously suggested that we live in a 'risk society' in which individuals are ever more conscious of self-produced or manufactured risk.[12] Although, it is debatable whether the world is 'more risky' or more objectively dangerous now than in the past, more possible outcomes in the world are now regarded as amenable to human decision and intervention, rather than being in the hands of the gods.[13] As part of a politics of uncertainty, publics of varying kinds demand decisions and the right to hold decision-makers to account. In this view, the problem is to render scientific and other experts accountable and their judgements publicly transparent. The public outcry over an alleged link between the MMR vaccine and autism in children, and the controversy surrounding the now discredited 'expert' testimony of Sir Roy Meadows in child protection cases, are two recent examples of this politics of uncertainty.

Secondary risk management

But the risk management of everything poses a different agenda of concern, namely that the experts who are being made increasingly accountable for what they do are now becoming more preoccupied with managing their own risks. Specifically, secondary risks to their reputation are becoming as significant as the primary risks for which experts have knowledge and training. This trend is resulting in a dangerous flight from judgement and a culture of defensiveness that create their own risks for organisations in preparing for, and responding to, a future they cannot know. It will be argued that a 'new politics of uncertainty' is required to counter this trend.

The argument

This essay seeks to describe the institutional shape of the risk management of everything, to understand its causes and to offer a critique with suggestions for future policy.

The arguments below are necessarily sweeping and focus largely on UK examples. Accordingly, their generalisability and comparability can be questioned. Much work remains to be done in order to understand the emerging institutionalisation of a new pervasive risk management through definitions, attributions of responsibility, communicative structures and accountability demands. It may well be that the UK context is an exceptional one, characterised by a string of major failures and an aggressive media.

In the next chapter, the risk management of everything is discussed in the context of the state's preoccupation with risk management. Two key themes are analysed: risk communication and reputation; and risk-based regulation. This is followed by a discussion of three critical aspects of the new risk management which have emerged from the private sector, and which are being imported and adapted by the state: the emergence of risk-based internal control and its role in redefining organisational governance and regulation; the invention of the category of 'operational' risk to name a diverse basket of threats to organisations; the emergence of the category of reputational (and ethical) risk and the manner in which corporate social responsibility agendas are being translated by risk management ideas.

From this descriptive anatomy of the new risk management, the argument seeks in chapter 6 to explain its appearance. It is suggested that, while the risk management of everything may be a fad, a more complete explanation appeals to an individualisation process which is driving risk experts and professionals to focus more on their personal, legal and reputational risks, rather than on the primary risks embodied in their formal mission. This pathology of risk management is further criticised in chapter 7 in terms of four overlapping problem areas: legalisation and trust; the imperialism of internal control; trust in risk numbers; and the privatisation of public policy.

In conclusion, the diagnosis provides suggestions for an 'intelligent risk management'[14] capable of avoiding these problems. There is also a plea for a new politics of uncertainty which could support the public conditions under which the worst side effects of our organisational obsession with risk and its management could be mitigated.

2. The state as risk manager

Modern states play a role that is easy to describe in risk management terms. They pool and redistribute certain types of risk via health and welfare systems. Since the nineteenth century they have produced legislation in a wide variety of areas. As regulatory states, they also create an increasing number of specific organisations charged with 'risk regulation'. In the UK it is possible to list the Health and Safety Executive, the Food Standards Agency, the Financial Services Authority, the Commission for Health Audit and Inspection and many other bodies. Although it is plausible to describe the state *as if* it had a risk management or insurance function in a general way, state and related organisations have only recently become self-conscious and explicit about risk and their risk management agendas, adopting concepts and standards from private sector blueprints. In the UK, risk management started to become part of the official self-description and self-understanding of central government activities in the late 1990s.

This growth of risk talk at the centre of government and in regulatory organisations may be explained in terms of a growing consciousness of risk to the state for failure to deliver on public services. It may also have something to do with public perceptions of the state as a source of risk in the face of mismanaged crises.

Research has shown that there is very considerable variety in the manner in which risks are processed by state agencies; the 'government of risk' is by no means uniform across problems and functions, with public perceptions, moral frameworks, institutional arrangements and the nature of the risk itself giving rise to variation in 'risk regulation regimes'.[15] Nevertheless, the new mood of risk in UK government reveals some common preoccupations which frame and organise ideas about the management of risk. Two themes deserve particular attention: communication with the public; and risk-based regulation.

Risk perception, communication and reputation
Risk perception
An extensive research literature on risk perception exists and the idea that individuals process and react to dangers in a wide variety of ways, dependent on many different features of how risk is framed and presented, is well established. From this point of view, individual attitudes to risk are far from being a given. Research has informed a critical project to question the exclusivity of scientific and expert authority. It challenges highly rationalistic models of risk analysis which assume away the important psychological and cultural dimensions of risk understanding. This critique, an early politics of uncertainty, has only very slowly and selectively been absorbed into mainstream regulatory thinking.

The 1992 Royal Society report on risk significantly included a number of these issues, but the synthesis between technical scientific conceptions of risk analysis and social–psychological analyses of risk perception was evidently an uneasy and imperfect one.[16] A later report in the USA was more successful in this integration,[17] and policy receptivity to risk perception issues has changed in the light of a number of public crises and scandals. From 1995 ideals of stakeholder engagement and the importance of communication began to figure prominently in generic risk management blueprints.

In the UK, the handling of the BSE crisis had a catalytic effect on government, forcing a recognition of the need to manage risk more explicitly.[18] In particular, risk communication was accepted as necessary to manage public expectation and its potential disappointments.

Risk communication

In recent years, risk communication ideas have become normalised in a number of UK policy documents, notably the Strategy Unit report in 2002 which has a separate chapter on 'handling and communicating' risks to the public. Earlier policy documents by the National Audit Office translated private sector enterprise risk management (ERM) ideas into the state domain. The UK Treasury has now adopted this agenda, establishing risk management guidelines for government departments, and supporting this with an educational and cultural change programme headed by 'risk improvement' managers (RIMs). In addition, the Treasury Risk Support Team has absorbed the work of the UK Interdepartmental Liaison Group on Risk Assessment (UK-ILGRA).[19]

This central government initiative in the UK has been described as one of 'organised paranoia'. It has the aim of improving the government's capacity to spot new risks in incubation. But it is also reminiscent of, and extends, reform processes begun by the new public management.[20] Risk is the new concept for challenging the quality of public services in the absence of real markets.

The widening enfranchisement of, and communication with, lay publics in the business of risk regulation is itself varied and the extent to which the process is democratic remains problematic.[21] There has been debate about the implications of participation and communication strategies for 'risk acceptance' processes. Previously, the sole preserve of expert committees and individuals, the emergence of demands for consultation and for taking seriously the views of diverse publics has brought the principles for accepting risk – 'risk appetite' in the language of private sector risk management standards – into public question.

Attitudes to risk vary across individuals, and may be different at different levels of an organisation.[22] Risk attitudes or appetites may also vary across different aspects of the same risk, may in reality not correspond to any stated appetite and may change with new or better information. Policy-makers seeking to aggregate these views before deciding whether or not to accept a risk therefore face many difficulties. Not least is the problem of knowing which public understandings of risk to take seriously and which not.[23] In some cases, the public may understand risk issues very clearly.

The democratisation of risk policy has also sustained a huge discussion to do with risk architecture and risk acceptance principles. The much discussed precautionary principle in its various forms places the burden of proof on any technological innovation, most prominently in the case of GM foods, to demonstrate its safety. Opponents of this principle argue for the importance of innovation and for the need for some kind of cost–benefit approach to risk acceptance.

Reputational risk to the state

By extending the scope of risk management practice beyond the domain of the expert, to embrace and somehow enfranchise lay views of risk, the state seeks to improve its capacity to handle risk. According to some commentators, given the indeterminacy of risk assessment it is essential that public perspectives play a role in the risk regulation process.[24] But the growing enfranchisement of publics and stakeholders in risk regulation regimes has much to do with managing the perceived *legitimacy* of regulatory activity and decisions. There is more than a hint that risk communication strategies are as concerned with managing the secondary or *reputational risk* to regulators, public bodies and government as they are about the primary risk that is to be regulated.

The UK government, like many others, is concerned to manage public expectations with improved service delivery and project management.[25] The gap between these expectations and actual performance constitutes a reputational, and ultimately political, risk for government and its agencies, such as regulatory bodies. Indeed, it has been argued that the creation of such bodies is itself a strategy by which government manages its reputational risk.[26]

Risk-based regulation and the politics of uncertainty

Over time it has become increasingly accepted that regulation is likely to be more effective and more acceptable if it works with the grain of private control systems. By harnessing private control activities for public regulatory purposes, regulatory organisations can be relieved of much of the economic and epistemic burden of detailed rule-making, and can focus on overseeing the design and functioning of local systems.[27]

Responsive models of regulation

This ideal model, which is variously described as 'enforced self-regulation', 'regulated self-regulation' and 'meta-regulation', gives internal control systems a central role.[28] Examples of the model are increasingly found in banking regulation (the Basel 2 reforms in particular), in health and safety regulation, in teaching quality regulation and many other areas. In theory, regulatory regimes can become more 'responsive' to the self-organisation of regulatees, whether these are banks or local government service providers. The self-control activities of organisations have become an essential component of regulatory agendas which are developing in the direction of 'risk-based regulation'. This is a blueprint for the risk management state.

In a number of domains regulatory bodies have explicitly adopted risk-based approaches to the organisation of resource allocation.[29] Risk-based regulation is part of being explicit about limited resources and the need to direct them to where they are needed most, eg failing schools, unsafe facilities, banks with weak controls. Risk-based approaches to regulation are simultaneously strategic and goal-oriented. This conjunction of risk and strategy is fundamental to the marketing of new approaches to regulation and risk management, in particular by creating a common vocabulary between regulator and regulated.

But why does this emerging change in the operating philosophy of regulatory bodies matter?

Risk-based regulation and the politics of uncertainty

Risk-based regulation is the potential site of a new 'politics of uncertainty', an idea discussed in more detail in the final chapter. Such a politics would be premised on the acceptance that failures and accidents are possible in complex environments, even with the most competent, ethical and expert oversight possible. Given the emphasis being placed on the importance of innovation to economic growth and prosperity, it might even be said that some failure is necessary.[30] Risk-based regulation necessarily embodies the idea that failures are possible. However, the degree to which regulators and politicians are able to be publicly explicit about this will vary according to the perceived reputational and political risks of doing so.

Political discourses of 'zero-tolerance' sit uneasily with a risk-based ethos. In addition, an event such as the demise of Equitable Life, which could be regarded as 'tolerable' from the impersonal point of view of systemic financial risk, was in fact experienced by large numbers of people as a life-changing catastrophe – and reflected in the media as such. People also feel differently about specific risks, eg public attitudes to deaths on the road differ from attitudes to deaths on public transport. All this means that *ex ante* public acceptance of the possibility of failure can never control *ex post* public reaction to actual failure.

The prospects for a new politics of uncertainty are also threatened because risk-based regulation can be used as part of regulators' own secondary or reputational risk management process. Indeed, regulatory organisations must handle the uncertainties and volatilities of the political environment – political risk. From this point of view, risk-based regulation is ambivalent. On the one hand it contains the seeds for a new risk politics; on the other it may exacerbate the risk management of everything.

The example of the UK General Medical Council (GMC) is instructive. The official inquiry into the serial murders by Harold Shipman exposed weaknesses and deficiencies in the GMC's regulatory practices, particularly its processes for the investigation of errors and administration of complaints, and its cultural bias in favour of doctors. At the time of writing it seems likely that there will be much greater formalisation of the 'fitness to practise' regulations for UK doctors. In a critical climate, a publicly explicit risk-based approach to the regulation of doctors is unlikely to be acceptable. However, it is likely that a new regime will in fact operate in this way. More importantly, the reforms will increase the burden of 'auditable process' in the medical field. The GMC is seeking to rebuild its regulatory reputation and doctors will intensify their personal risk management strategies. Whether any of this would have prevented any or all of the Shipman murders is an unknown.

Summary

The regulatory state is becoming a risk management state. Operating in an indirect manner, states are trading depth for breadth in their operations, functioning via an enormous variety of risk regulation regimes. Although there is considerable cross-sectional variation in practices, two key themes are evident: an increasing emphasis on communication with different publics as a basis for managing reputation; and a trend for more explicitly risk-based approaches to regulation and control in a widening number of areas. Above all, the risk management state depends on internal control systems in organisations which proceduralise risk.

3. Turning organisations inside out

internal control becomes risk management

A conspicuous feature of the risk management of everything has been the rise of the internal control system. Such systems translate primary or real risks into systems risks, such as early warning mechanisms and compliance violation alerts. Thus many risks can be, and are being, operationalised as organisational processes of control, eg BSE and farm management systems, GM crops and traceability systems, earthquakes and emergency services/building regulations, terrorism and the organisation of security and intelligence services. Clinical risk management was originally conceptualised in terms of accidental harms done to patients during the care delivery process; it has subsequently become part of a regulatory regime concerned with the effectiveness of health care in general, a matter of health care organisation rather than specific clinicians.[31] Indeed, risk management was one of the five pillars of clinical governance informing the work of the Commission for Health Improvement in the UK (now replaced by the Commission for Health Audit and Inspection).[32]

Organisational translations of risk into internal controls are necessary conditions of possibility for risk-based regulation, and hence for the successful operation of the risk management state. Internal control is thereby the state in organisational miniature.

The topic of internal control in organisations is hardly likely to set the pulses racing. Indeed, for many years this subject has been a private matter for managers, a dry technical domain of control specialists with checklists, evaluation questionnaires and a whole host of other instruments. Internal control could even be described as a kind of organisational common sense. Entities as diverse as private corporations, corner shops, clubs and churches all require minimum financial and non-financial control systems to keep track of money and related activities. But far from being a private organisational matter, the effectiveness of internal control systems is now an issue for public policy and formal law.[33] In short, *private* internal control has come to play a very significant external *public* role; organisations ranging from major companies to universities are being turned 'inside out' in its name, and this more than anything else drives a risk management explosion which demands the externalisation and justification of organisational control arrangements.

A brief history of internal control

The transformation in the position and status of internal control began in the 1980s in the financial services sector and became more pronounced and generic during the 1990s. A critical event in the UK was the collapse of the Maxwell empire and subsequent reactions which led to the publication of the Cadbury Code on Corporate Governance in 1992.[34] Corporate governance, traditionally understood in the context of markets for corporate control, became reconceptualised as a matter of internal organisational structure and design. The Cadbury Code, though formally voluntary, established the principle that senior management are responsible for the maintenance of an internal control system. The general principles in the UK code, and its subsequent refinements, have been hugely influential, shaping generic initiatives elsewhere, including at the transnational level.[35] In the USA, a parallel critical event was the publication of the COSO document on internal control, following a congressional inquiry into fraudulent financial reporting.[36] Internal control was redefined broadly to cover not just controls relating to financial accounting, the typical focus of auditors, but also regulatory compliance matters and operations more generally. This expansion and formalisation of the internal control agenda was crucial, and the COSO legacy is evident in subsequent guidance documents, particularly the Turnbull Report in the UK.

Another important source of thinking about internal control has been the development of standards for quality assurance and management systems.[37] The significance of this quality assurance model cannot be underestimated; it has been exported to a wide variety of domains and organisational settings, not least teaching quality assurance in UK universities. Such systems have been criticised for being excessively bureaucratic and for concentrating on auditable process rather than on substantive outputs and performances. Worse still, they distract professionals from core tasks and create incentives for gaming.

The elements of the quality assurance template have been expanded further in the direction of generic risk management standards. In 1995, the first national level risk management standard was published jointly by Australia and New Zealand. This has been followed by standards in Canada, the UK and Japan.[38] Common to all these different efforts to standardise the risk management process is a linkage between risk management and strategic objectives. This conceptualisation seeks to elevate the internal control function from its lowly historical position to the top of a risk management process which is enterprise-wide in ambition because it addresses the risks to the objectives of the enterprise as a whole.[39]

The changing meaning of internal control

Why has internal control become so public and why this mutation as risk management?

A first answer is to be found in changing ideas of regulation discussed in the previous chapter.

A second answer is to be found in the domain of insurance and in challenges to the logic of risk transfer. Large companies have become more critical of their insurance strategies, preferring to retain and self-manage many risks, which they might have previously transferred. Companies like BP Amoco began to realise in the 1990s that they were paying too much for insurance and others have discovered the benefits of consolidating hitherto separate insurance lines.[40] At the same time, these organisations have become more aware of individual risks at the core of their businesses which do not lend themselves to easy pricing from an insurance point of view. Reputational and political risks have begun to occupy management attention as never before, further fuelling the tendency to look critically at insurance as being only one part of a broad enterprise risk management (ERM) strategy. From this point of view, ERM emerges *as a form of self-insurance in its own right*, and self-insurance provides incentives to invest in control systems.

A third answer is to be found in a distinctive form of institutional response to crisis and scandal which demands new conditions of 'risk auditability' and transparency for organisations. Risk auditing has a long history dating back to the 1980s in the so-called hazard industries, where the International Safety Rating System created the conditions for 'risk inspection'.[41] Primary risks themselves may not be amenable to auditing or direct inspection, but the organisational control systems through which such risks are represented can be. In this way, the auditing and public control of risk is achieved indirectly via the inspection of management systems of control. So, the rise of internal control is part of a macro- and micro-level politics of responding to crisis by creating new risk accountability structures supporting chains of public and private reassurance. From this point of view, the risk management of everything seems little different in principle from the audit explosion.

Summary

The risk-based internal control system has become an increasingly significant regulatory object, particularly with the passing of the Sarbanes-Oxley Act in the USA, and regulatory incentives exist to have 'good' internal controls in a wide variety of areas: solvency and capital adequacy, health care, safety, environment, business continuity, teaching, waste management and so on. The private world of organisational internal control systems has been turned inside out, made public, codified and standardised and repackaged as risk management. In this way, a blueprint for extending the reach of risk management into every aspect of organisational life has been created. Internal control systems are also highly problematic. Not only is it difficult to define their effectiveness, which is in principle unknowable, but, more crucially, a growing obsession with internal control (a mutation of the earlier audit explosion) may itself be a source of risk. First, internal control systems are organisational projections of controllability which may be misplaced; such systems are only as good as the imaginations of those who designed them.[42] Second, internal control systems are essentially inward-looking and may embody mistaken assumptions of what the public really wants reassurance about. Risk management and certifications of the effectiveness of internal control systems may do little to enhance public trust in senior management of organisations. While practitioners are well aware of the limitations of these systems, 'better' control systems continue to be regarded as politically acceptable solutions to crisis, even where it is well known that such systems would not have prevented the crisis in question. The invention of the category of operational risk provides an example.

4. Anxiety and classification

the invention of operational risk[43]

The risk management of everything involves the creation of new risk categories for managerial and political attention. A specific illustration is the emergence of the category of operational risk in banking and insurance as a label for a number of real but 'awkward' risks facing organisations. Industry mythology associates operational risk with a specific event, namely the collapse of Barings bank in 1995 resulting from the activities of the rogue trader Nick Leeson. In reality, the category of operational risk pre-existed the collapse of Barings and was used in the context of more humble and less dramatic risks associated with organisational infrastructure and systems.[44] But it was the Barings experience which helped to sell the idea within many organisations. The category of operational risk became a prominent focus for organisational reform and discussion despite being problematic to define.

Operational risk as a 'boundary object'

The definition of operational risk settled upon by the Basel Committee, the transnational policy body for banking supervision, is very general: the risk of direct or indirect loss resulting from inadequate or failed internal processes, people and systems or from external events.[45] The broad nature of this definition means that the concept of operational risk can appeal to a wide range of sub-groups within organisations and functions as an umbrella for many different interests. Such concepts function as 'boundary objects', which link the interests of diverse expert communities.[46] From this point of view, operational risk has served to organise the risk management field, creating an apparent unity from diverse elements and directing managerial attention in a new and systematic way to a portfolio of dangers and uncertainties. Indeed, the story of operational risk characterises a new risk management in which the imperative is to make visible and manageable essentially unknowable and incalculable risks. New categories are a part of the appearance of manageability, a conceptual 'mopping-up' exercise involving definitions and formalisations.

Implementation

Operational risk is principally focused on fraud and infrastructure risk issues, but the implementation process under the Basel 2 proposals remains controversial. Much discussion has taken place about what constitutes an operational risk 'event' (actual loss, possible loss, a near miss?). Furthermore, the case of Barings suggests that significant operational risk events, eg uncontrolled employees, are high impact and low probability. By their very nature these events lack rich historical data sets and exist at the limits of manageability. However, a great deal of operational risk management activity in financial institutions in fact focuses on routine systems errors and malfunctions. In many cases it is as if organisational agents, faced with the task of inventing a management practice, have chosen a pragmatic path of collecting data which is collectable, rather than that which is necessarily relevant. In this way, operational risk management in reality is a kind of displacement. The burden of managing unknowable risks, a Nick Leeson, is replaced by an easier task which can be successfully reported to seniors.

The invention of the category of operational risk within banking illustrates how new concerns and anxieties may drive the risk management of everything. The case shows how categories and classifications are significant in the organisational displacement of radical uncertainty (rogue traders, murdering doctors) into something describable and, in aspiration, manageable. Killer events and sources of fear become translated into routines, regulations and data collection processes; anxiety, as the secondary risk of attempting to manage the unmanageable, is 'tamed' by a kind of naming.

Operational risk management as a myth of control

The policy question is whether operational risk specifically, and internal control in general, really stimulate an intelligent risk management capable of challenging existing ways of making sense of the world within and outside organisations, or whether they simply end up as the 'normalisation of deviance' in a dense network of procedures and routines. The suspicion is that, while operational risk facilitates a greater 'managerialisation of risk' via new organisational processes, and extends the scope of the risk manager's and the regulator's work into more corners of organisational and social life, it also reinforces myths of controllability in areas where this is at best limited – for example, the senior management culture and the often discussed 'tone at the top' of organisations. Much the same can be said of reputational risk management.

5. What's in a name?

reputational risk and the transformation of social responsibility

The risk management of everything is characterised by the emergence of secondary or reputational risk management.

Reputational and secondary risk

A simple example shows the difference between primary and secondary risks. Assume that the directors of a very large public company consistently incur, and do not pay personally, parking fines for their company cars. The primary risk to the company, in this case of financial loss, is probably very small in relation to its annual turnover. Accountants and auditors would say that these amounts are *not material*, should not be separately disclosed in the annual report and should be 'lost' in general expenses. But what would the public think of this behaviour by corporate leaders? How would the media report it if it came to light? Indeed, what general signals of corporate trustworthiness would this give? Herein lies the secondary or reputational risk for the organisation. Reputation has turned the concept of materiality upside down; financially immaterial events may have huge potential significance for the organisation. The management of such risks demands attention to the deepest operating assumptions of organisations.

Background

Although, the concept of 'reputation' as an intangible 'asset' has long been recognised and formalised in economics, it only became a prominent practical and managerial category in the mid-1990s. Indeed, as in the case of operational risk, 1995 was also a significant year for the emergence of 'reputational risk' as a category of organisational and individual attention.

The birth of a discipline of 'reputational management' can be traced to the now famous experiences of Shell in the wake of its decision to dispose of the Brent Spar oil platform in the North Sea.[47] Despite having considered the environmental impact options carefully, Shell failed to take account of likely public opinion about water-based disposal, and the ability of prominent environmental lobby groups to influence public perceptions, resulting in widespread boycotting of Shell products and outlets. The event revealed the power of external groups, assisted by the media, to threaten the legitimacy and value of a large multinational organisation.[48] The Shell organisation survived this event (and criticism of its role in Nigeria), although it underwent a profound internal reorganisation as a consequence. More recently, it has suffered adverse publicity for overstating its oil reserves.

Another well-trodden example concerns the professional services firm of Arthur Andersen which collapsed following revelations about its role in the demise of Enron. The local actions of a small number of individuals, and the shredding of documents, were able to bring into question the legitimacy of the entire global organisation to practise audits. This seems to have happened because these specific actions were also regarded as reflecting a systemic or cultural feature of the larger firm. Timing was also critical: coinciding with the audit renewal season, clients left and the firm was effectively doomed.

Institutionalisation and amplication

The two cases dramatise how certain events may be *amplified* by social and institutional forces beyond the control of individuals and organisations. The media is an important source of amplification, notwithstanding the damage to its own reputation and credibility in the UK during 2004. The 'secondary effects' of an original risk event can have very real consequences[49] and the existence of reputational risk management reflects a belief that amplification effects can be explicitly managed and attenuated. Strategies such as swift remedial action, eg product recall, have been well known for some time, but have now been drawn into the orbit of risk management. The growth of interest in reputation has also been an opportunity for public relations departments and officers to stake a claim in the risk management process.[50] It has also coincided with, and reinforced, the increasing recognition of the importance of 'new economy' intangible sources of organisational value at risk, and the necessity of enfranchising external groups and interests, commonly known as stakeholders, in organisational processes and decision-making.

The institutionalisation of the category of reputational risk by a panoply of evangelical consultants has provided a new focus for both private and public organisations on the relational dimensions of their activities, on new types of asset and liability, and on their embeddedness in networks and communities. At Barclays Bank, which was criticised for many years for its South African interests, there is now a 'brand and reputation committee' which puts reputational risk on a par with operational and other risks, and which unites the heads of risk, investor relations, public policy and marketing and communications.[51] Reputational risk and its management now cut across traditionally separate functional domains in organisations.

Like operational risk, 'reputation' also functions as a 'boundary object' linking hitherto compartmentalised and distinct interests, such as public relations, accounting for intangibles and corporate social responsibility. Indeed, the most significant impact of the rise of reputation as a management category has been its role in aligning various corporate social responsibility (CSR) agendas with risk management, namely by making a wide variety of social issues, which might ordinarily be externalised and forgotten by organisations, imaginable as having a potentially significant internal impact.

From this point of view, reputational risk management means the rationally self-interested recognition of the risks posed by various agents in the organisational environment. In contrast to hopes for a new corporate ethics involving greater stakeholder dialogue and communication, risk management standards seem to represent stakeholders primarily as a source of external risk to be understood and managed.[52] Corporate social responsibility is thereby a form of secondary risk management.

Defending reputation

The defensive dimension of reputation management is understandable in the face of greater 'anti-capitalist' popular activism, organised and resourced consumer groups, and a global media system capable of transforming minor local transgressions into major crises. Reputational risk management has also become a critical dimension of legal risk management; relatively minor fines, such as for parking mentioned above, can lead to exacerbated reputational damage. This places 'legal risk' in a new space of organisational concern, broader than the direct economic cost of fines and settlements. The appearance of ethics and legal risk officers is a response to this.

Following a line of reasoning developed by the sociologist Ulrich Beck, the rise of reputational risk represents a shift in power from corporations to 'unpredictable consumers', who are increasingly able to reverse burdens of proof about product safety and quality and to amplify these issues. But in the face of highly organised public groups and NGOs, organisations may be *over-responsive* to public concerns. Indeed, reputational risk management practice may itself be part of the amplification of reputational risk, with organisations unable or unwilling to contest public perceptions of their actions.[53]

The 1990s witnessed extensive attacks on the character of business and the professions in the UK and overseas. In such a climate, risk management in general and reputation management in particular are attractive solutions to the problem of legitimacy. Coupled to mantras that social responsibility is good business, they seem to provide a solution to the problem of public trust consistent with existing ways of operating. Yet, this is questionable.

There is something deeply paradoxical about being public about 'managing' reputation compared with committing to substantive changes in performance. The more one is perceived to be attempting to manage public perceptions, the less successful this must be. Nevertheless, reputation has emerged as a new management object for private and public sector organisations, naming a domain of exposure and anxiety where organisational identity and economic survival are at stake. Reputation may be a poor diagnostic category but, like operational risk, it plays a role in the organisation of managerial attention and in the creation of new processes and functions.

And if everything may impact on organisational reputation, then reputational risk management demands the risk management of everything.

6. Explaining the risk management of everything

function, fashion and fear

Previous chapters have suggested that the risk management of everything is a story of the metamorphosis of internal control and regulation. It involves an intensified emphasis on risk communication and the management of reputation for both state sector and private organisations. New categories, such as operational risk, have emerged to absorb a whole series of disparate organisational concerns under the banner of risk management. In the private sector, there is the promise of an all-embracing enterprise risk management process derived in linear, machine-like fashion from the highest strategic objectives of the organisation. In the public sector, risk management is becoming the new basis for challenging and defining the parameters of service provision in a wide range of areas, and for organising the allocation of scarce regulatory resources.

But why has risk management become such a dominant organising model, for private and public organisations and for governments? And why, given all this effort, is there something deeply unconvincing and un-reassuring about these efforts?

Explaining the new risk management
Function
A functional explanation for the phenomenon suggests that the emergence of a systematic, generic and broad approach to risk

management is a *rational* response to the fact that the environment of individuals and organisations, indeed the world, has become genuinely 'more risky'. So, the arguments runs, financial markets have become more volatile, organisational activities have become more dangerous with ever greater negative externalities, new large-scale threats exist from epidemics, from terrorism, from climate change. Individual states are ever weaker to control their destinies in a system of global interconnectedness, while technology advances to create both new opportunities and threats (GM foods, nanotechnology). The image is of a 'runaway world' in need of new forms of risk governance.[54] In such a world, the reinvention of risk management and its repositioning as a critical model of good organisational control seems a natural response. It is reinforced and justified by each new dramatic headline event, from Barings to Enron and Parmalat, from Challenger to Columbia, from BSE to mobile phones, and from 11 September 2001 to 11 March 2004 (the date of the Madrid train bombings).

Versions of this argument have become part of a managerial and political rhetoric, but this is not to say that the arguments themselves are true. The risk management of everything may well have some of the rational functional response characteristics mentioned above (universities, for example, do seem to operate in a more uncertain funding environment than in the past), but evidence that the world is more risky or dangerous is at best equivocal. Furthermore, there is nothing particularly *natural* or obvious about the new organisation and scope of risk management. Some risks and dangers receive more attention than others. Organisational leaders seem to be particularly preoccupied with reputational risk. Accordingly, we must look to an explanation of the risk management of everything in *institutions*. As the concept of the social amplification of risk suggests, under-standings of risk are mediated and constructed by institutions such as the media and law.[55] In addition, institutional responses are very much guided by cultural demands for control, accountability and responsibility attribution.

The visibility or otherwise afforded to certain events by the world media (11 September 2001 compared with the Toulouse factory explosion ten days later) and political attention systems are critical in determining the profile of issues. Not all events that might be publicly registered as crises, accidents or disasters become so. The processing of risk will be influenced by institutional possibilities for making decisions and allocating responsibility for historical and future outcomes.[56] We need to understand the contingent and conditioned nature by which critical events are processed by institutions. How actual and possible events are perceived, classified, dramatised, made visible and mobilised will determine their relevance for risk management agendas, as the case of reputational risk demonstrated. From this point of view, the primary question to be answered is not 'has the world become riskier?' but 'what are the collective mechanisms by which some risks become managerially and politically visible while others do not?'.

Risk management as fashion

One answer to this question points to the new risk management as a managerial and administrative *fashion*. In the UK we might call this the 'Turnbullisation' of organisational life. It has been suggested that three conditions underlie the creation of new managerial models: the collapse of a previous fashion, a widespread performance gap and a new rhetoric emphasising this gap and offering an enhanced organisational rationality.[57] Crises and accidents have often been diagnosed in terms of poor, non-integrated risk management, particularly in the context of large projects. A performance gap has been constructed by multiple surveys of 'deficient' practice, and a new risk management is promoted via management consultants and related agents operating through conferences, professional networks, business press circuits and business schools. New models of operational and reputational risk management are presented as rational and natural, although it may be that 'in part to inflate their own status within organisations and to expand the markets for their service, the professions created the impression of [. . .] much greater threat. . .'[58]

This 'fashion-based' explanation should not be overstated, but it is undoubtedly the case that professionals of varying kinds play an important role in reconstructing the conceptual architecture of risk management, making it readily portable and diffusible as a model of best practice (witness the reframing and selling of business continuity planning in the wake of 11 September and the renewed emphasis on resilience since then[59]).

A further important rhetorical component of this strategy has been the need to demonstrate the business case for risk management, a claim which litters conference papers and the professional press. Critical events are not only categorised as crises and failure, but as threats to business and/or organisational survival in one form or another. In the process of selling new management ideas promulgators walk a tightrope between the need to emphasise both their novelty and their status as business common sense. Hence the impression given by many risk management blueprints is that they are simply a new fashionable name for an old model. Business and public sector professionals readily admit that if risk management is not already part of the organisational business model, buying it off the shelf merely for compliance purposes is unlikely to help.

Making risk auditable

The fashion-based explanation by itself is inadequate. Fads succeed because they are able to appeal to deep-seated fears, aspirations and values. So the risk management of everything has a deeper basis of explanation as a continuation of control and accountability ambitions begun by the audit explosion.[60]

A conspicuous feature of the expanded risk management already noted above is the convergence of risk management and corporate governance, evident in the early 1990s in a programme to position derivatives trading in a wider management control framework.[61] Risk management has grown from a limited role in vetoing particular transactions to become synonymous with being a well-governed organisation, which is internally and externally accountable for how it 'handles' uncertainty. This demand for the governance of the unknowable requires organisational proceduralisation, something started by the audit explosion and reflected in the generic flavour of risk-based controls.[62] Although marketed in the name of outcomes, strategy, value and best business practice, the cultural biases that drive the new risk management demand a procedural and auditable set of practices because control must be made increasingly publicly visible and because organisational responsibility must be made transparent. In such a cultural environment, with institutions which tend to amplify blame and the logic of compensation, it is rational for organisations and the agents within them to invest in management systems with a strong secondary risk flavour.

But why has the cultural environment which drives defensive risk management come about?

Individualisation, litigation and fear

A full answer to this question is beyond the scope of this essay but would point to the growing individualisation of modern society, and the rise of consumer and other claimant-type rights in a wide variety of areas. This has created a more demanding context for organisations and drives an emphasis on stakeholder communication issues at the expense of trust in experts, specialists and professions. The increasing enfranchisement of the public via active representative organisations provides an environment of potential legal and critical claims, which constitute a risk to organisations – this is partially reflected in the rise of what some might call a litigation or compensation culture. However, as the recent history of the UK General Medical Council shows, failure to include non-expert representation in governance mechanisms is also risky.

A wider set of risks and dangers facing individuals is being increasingly perceived as 'involuntary', imposed by business and public organisations who must be made responsible. Indeed, if all risks were thought of in this way, all law would be compensatory law.[63] It may be that a growing understanding of many risks as involuntary and compensatable provides the cultural climate for the social amplification of risk and for the increasing legalisation of organisational life. Trips have become risky for schools who need to demonstrate that they have taken all reasonable steps to ensure the safety of pupils. Even if such trips are not curtailed (schools cannot easily 'exit' from this activity), the climate in which they are undertaken has created a risk management issue both to protect the pupils, the primary risk, but also to protect the school's name and that of staff, the secondary risk.

From this point of view, the primary driver of the risk management of everything has nothing to do with organisational efficiency, although it will be marketed in this way. Rather, it arises from the increasingly defensive mood of agents who previously absorbed risk on behalf of others. These risk management agents – auditors, insurers, the state, doctors, teachers and anyone else exercising a judgement on behalf of others – have become preoccupied with their own risks, particularly in media and law-intense environments. Coupled to institutionalised assumptions and myths about the manageability of risks, there is an intensification of strategies to avoid blame when things go wrong.

The risks of the risk management of everything

The risk management of everything reflects the efforts of organisational agents previously engaged in the collectivisation and pooling of social and economic risks to offload and re-individualise their own personal risk. The result is a potentially catastrophic downward spiral in which expert judgement shrinks to an empty form of defendable compliance. In this way the risk management of everything poses major risks to a society in which the most pressing and most unpredictable problems cannot be solved without the effective marshalling of expert knowledge and judgement. The remainder of this essay considers what might be done about it.

7. Out of control?

avoiding the risks of risk management

Crises and disasters have been important pressures for change in risk management and risk regulation:

○ the collapse of the Maxwell empire initiated the UK corporate governance reforms which turned organisations 'inside out', and the focus on internal control systems is being taken to a further extreme by the Sarbanes-Oxley Act;

○ problems at Shell in the 1990s effectively gave birth to reputational management, and operational risk took off in the wake of the collapse of Barings bank;

○ there has been a surge of interest in business continuity and organisational resilience and now terrorism risk management is high on the public agenda.

Governments are also adopting explicit risk management frameworks as a response to poorly managed large projects.

Relevant to all these examples is the idea of a 'man-made disaster', a concept which focuses attention on the organisational and managerial processes which 'incubate' the disaster or crisis.[64] In most cases, a point supported by a telling analysis of the Challenger space shuttle launch decision, relevant risk information is available but not acted upon because of deep-seated organisational assumptions.[65]

Although easy to note in retrospect, many disasters exhibit a common pattern of failure to appreciate and process information, particularly anomalous information that does not fit habitual channels of data processing, eg gossip. On the basis of 'incubation theory', the starting point for serious disaster analysis must be the 'notional normality' embodied in routine patterns of activity which inhibit intelligent risk processing. From this point of view, crises and catastrophes do not just happen suddenly; they are in an important sense 'organised' and have their origins in failures of management and intelligence processes over a long period of time. Even apparently surprise or random acts (the terrorist attacks of 11 September 2001; the Turkish earthquake) are being traced to historical organisational and intelligence failures (fragmentation in security and police services; non-compliance with construction regulations).

In the light of incubation theory, a risk management approach focused on organisational processes, such as enterprise risk management (ERM) and its variants, seems rational and functional. And yet, as suggested above, an intensified concern for organisational process may also incubate risks of its own, not least the failure to see, imagine or act upon the 'bigger picture'. Take the example of the auditor who discovered a major fraud because he noticed that a purchase invoice was not folded. Audit procedures include methods for vouching for the arithmetical accuracy of such documents, for agreeing the numbers to the accounts, and for agreeing the 'independent' nature of the invoice. But no amount of such process could allow one to see what this auditor saw; that if an invoice is not folded it probably did not arrive by post. And why would this be significant? Enquiries later revealed that it was being fraudulently constructed by the company to create a fictitious transaction. An auditor concerned solely with official process would not see the purchase invoice in this larger way, a vignette for how risk management processes can be risky.

Four related policy themes can be suggested for an analysis of the risks of risk management: legalisation and blame; the imperialism of internal control; trust in numbers; risk management as a private moral order.

Legalisation and blame

It was suggested above that, despite extensive claims to the contrary, the risk management of everything has its roots in defensive strategies by agents operating in highly legalised environments. However, this is not to make a universal claim about 'risk aversity' across all organisations and agents, as some commentators suggest.

Responsibility aversity

The phenomeonon is much more complex than this and relates not to *risk* aversity as such, but more to *responsibility* aversity. The distinction between primary and secondary risks helps to make the point. It may well be that in some cases and at some times, concerns with secondary risk management of reputation may engender risk aversity. In the school trips example, this would be the case if it could be shown that a school was withdrawing from providing such activities because of fear of litigation (rather than cost, teacher competence, etc). In the case of financial auditing, there is some anecdotal evidence that firms are shedding 'high-risk' clients – the very ones which should be thoroughly and competently audited. However, it is equally likely that first-order risk-takers will carry on as before but will be inclined to invest more heavily in second-order reputation- and legal-risk management.

In cultural environments where there is an asymmetry between the giving of blame and credit, it is perfectly consistent to have a high appetite for risk, because of the attraction of positive outcomes, and a low appetite for responsibility and blame in the face of negative outcomes. In short, the risk management of everything amplifies responsibility aversity across a wide range of possible risk appetites. It is the specific dynamics of these amplification processes in society, rather than any generalised aversion to risk-taking at the individual level, which potentially inhibits organisational innovation.[66]

Defensive proceduralism

Like the audit explosion before it, the new style of internal control-focused risk management has created an intensified attention to process, and to the responsibilities of middle managers who must constantly create appearances of process, via risk mapping and other techniques, in order to defend the rationality of their decisions. Where this 'risk game' is closely bound up with a 'blame game', the effect can be highly defensive reactions from organisational participants.[67] For example, in the face of new reporting responsibilities and sanctions for professionals relating to money laundering regulations, a wave of 'defensive reporting' is being anticipated as a risk management strategy.[68] The net effect will be to reduce dramatically the usefulness of the regulations, because authorities may be so overwhelmed with information that they are unable to process it effectively. Here the dynamics can be hinted at using the example of employment references.

Assume that, a bit like auditors, I have a statutory duty to give employment references for my students. As the perceived risks of litigation resulting from the giving of such references goes up, the content will tend to be restricted to factual data capable of clear verification; no opinion will be offered. As this practice takes hold, the value of references for information purposes will go down and will be sought for formal reasons (to defend a decision to employ taken on other grounds) or not sought at all. In both cases, the risk to the writer of the reference may actually go down because of the way it has been devalued. As a result, society will have more of what it does not really need – certifications and non-opinions which are commonly accepted as useless and which are time-consuming and distracting to produce – and less of what it does need – valuable but vulnerable judgements based on the best available knowledge to inform decisions in the face of uncertainty. This is the essential pathology of the risk management of everything.

The defensive preoccupation with reputational and legal risks which can dominate the climate of the risk management process has little to do with any direct possibility of legal action. Rather, there is evidence that legal initiatives in organisational environments get filtered in ways that are amenable to managerial agendas.[69] Thus, legal and other norms get embedded into organisational routines not because the real risks of litigation are well understood, but because the mere possibility creates a defensive orientation towards the need to justify decisions in retrospect. Accordingly, records are maintained in a particular form both for possible legal consumption, but also for internal defensive purposes.

From this point of view, the traditional distinction between legal regulation, voluntary codes and organisation-specific rules is not useful; all are effectively experienced by organisational participants 'legalistically' and demand defensive compliance strategies.[70] Even the well-worn distinction between principles and rules does not offer a solution path here; principles will tend to be interpreted legalistically in organisations via in-house manuals, training courses and clarificatory memos.

Consequences of defensive risk management

The consequences of defensive record-keeping for professional judgement are potentially catastrophic. By 'professional' judgement is meant a culture which accepts and understands that such specialised judgements may turn out in retrospect to be wrong, but which if made conscientiously and responsibly are not necessarily blameworthy. Already, concepts of 'defensive' medicine and auditing are spoken of, signalling a withdrawal of individual judgement from the public domain. Minimal records are kept, staff are cautioned about the use of email, and normal correspondence is littered with disclaimer paragraphs.

A society of 'small print'

Not only references for employment purposes but all forms of public opinion formation are a major casualty of this tendency, becoming less and less informative as it becomes more risky to venture a judgement. Despite bold claims for the value-adding potential of risk management, the deeper logic is that of compliance, bordering on paranoia and hyper-defensiveness. As risk language becomes legitimate in organisations, anything can be a risk demanding attention. And, in this downward spiral, it follows that employees and individuals become their own individualised, defensive risk managers in forms of responsibility aversion and a 'culture of fear' of secondary risk.[71]

Organisational agents can make risky choices in these legalised environments. In the case of the Soham murders, the failure to take up the employment references of Ian Huntley had catastrophic and tragic consequences. But in a cultural climate in which such references increasingly have little value, potential employers often do not follow them up. More generally, professionals are often so busy that they can only cope by taking a calculated risk *not* to implement certain procedures. Society is obliged to allocate blame when things go wrong, but these risky actions are also understandable.

A social contract at risk

It would be naïve to suppose that the defensiveness associated with risk management can be addressed overnight, either by changes in the law or in an intensification of claims that risk management is about value. Take the specific case of financial auditing as an example. Auditors in the UK are required to give an opinion for the benefit of the shareholders of a company as to whether the accounts show a 'true and fair' view. These reports tend to be short with 'boilerplate' descriptions of the audit process. The opinion only means as much as the terms of art through which it is expressed. Auditors know much more of course, and could in principle say more publicly. But they argue that without some relief from exposure to unlimited liability, it is rational for their public reports to be cautious and coded.

One can argue that there is a deep social contract whereby professions like accountants were granted monopolies over certain areas of work in return for providing a risk management service deemed important for the smooth operation of the economy. Today that contract seems fragile because the professions are preoccupied with avoiding risk to themselves. Consequently, audit reports and many other similar forms of public statement of opinion are much less valuable than they might be.

The policy challenge is to recognise that blame cultures and the legalisation of organisations in which they thrive may have little to do with real legal exposure as such, but are the result of years of 'hard-wiring' caution into the procedures and routines of risk management practices. This means that the problem is more managerial than legal, and concerns a reflex which, by taking on the clothes of law in its manuals and operating procedures, amplifies internal proceduralism. Changing legal systems will do little to change this; only challenging the real, as opposed to the official, mechanics of blame and reward can do this. And for this, a new politics of uncertainty is required.

Internal control: a new imperialism

Although an internal control revolution lies at the heart of the risk management explosion, process-based risk management and internal control systems suffer inherently from the problem of demonstrating their own effectiveness, despite upbeat claims and continuing attempts to recast control activity as a value proposition. Claims for risk management effectiveness involve risk agents in hard work to secure resources for their own departments by representing what they do as valuable. External crises make the case for risk-based internal control easier, raising it to the position of an almost untouchable principle, rather like auditing in the 1980s. Indeed, risk-based internal control has become a dominant image and representation of organisations, further reinforced by the Sarbanes-Oxley Act, which makes it an all-pervasive organisational, legal and regulatory principle which will expand well beyond its US jurisdiction. To lack internal controls, or to have a defective internal control system, is to fail as a legitimate organisation.

The consequences of imperial control

This position of internal control systems, the 'Turnbullisation' of organisational life in the UK, constitutes a profound risk of risk management. The obsession with risk-based internal control systems threatens to overwhelm other organisational functions. Internal control as an imperial principle (no one can be against it!) occupies the space where the regulatory state casts its shadow. Its dry, technical and unassuming history should not blind us to its profound consequences as an institutionalised mode of organising the handling of uncertainty. To a large extent internal control blueprints are fantasy policy documents, which project comforting images of controlling the uncontrollable.

Despite explicitly stated principles of supporting managed risk-taking and value creation, the deeper bureaucratic logic of internal control represents the opposite. To the extent that internal control-based risk management is over-organised, it is a kind of new religion and may encourage perverse behaviours by virtue of the faith it engenders in itself.[72] Furthermore, reliance on internal control may increase risk if it results in under-investment in risk intelligence elsewhere.

Towards an 'intelligent' risk management

The policy challenge is to put internal control and risk management in its place, in particular to create a legitimate, 'safe haven' for the judgement of the individual within an 'intelligent' risk management capable of confronting complex systems which may be out of control.[73] Judgement would be safe in the sense that mistakes can be made, or rather an intelligent view of 'mistake' could be taken allowing for the conjecture and refutation that are essential to progress and learning, and allowing for what it was reasonable to know at the time of a decision, rather than what is known with the benefit of hindsight.

At worst internal control systems 'imprison' risk management in a pretence of control, rather than enabling risk management to become a mechanism for encountering issues, including the problem of control itself.[74] The policy and managerial challenge is to attenuate and dampen the tendency for control systems to provide layers of pseudo-comfort about risk. There is a need to design soft management systems capable of addressing uncomfortable uncertainties and deep-seated working assumptions, overcoming the psychological and institutional need to fit recalcitrant phenomena into well-tried, incrementally adjusted, linear frameworks of understanding.

This agenda will require a new kind of risk expert, mathematically erudite perhaps but also the author of a wider organisational *narrative* of risk which sits above formal control systems. Managerial certifications, and auditor certification of these certifications, are the very antithesis of an intelligent, honest and experimental politics of uncertainty at the organisational level. They constitute a risk in themselves, a dumbing down and palliative in the face of the essential disorder of organisational life.

What kind of risk expert might this be? In the private sector the risk officer with varying degrees of seniority is particularly visible in the financial services sector and in large complex corporate organisations. In time, we could expect this role to become prominent in universities, hospitals and other public organisations.[75] But do such roles exacerbate the imperialism of internal control or, like the ideal communist state, will they wither away once they have served their purpose?

The chief risk officer

Officerships are themselves distinctive forms of cultural and organ- isational solution to problems. The label 'officer' endows any role with a seriousness and officialdom that it might not ordinarily have. The idea of a risk officer is nothing particularly unusual. It can be added to a long list which includes compliance officers, health and safety officers, information officers and knowledge officers. A 'chief ignorance officer' has even been half seriously proposed.[76] Some of these roles come and go, such as that of the 'chief operating officer', which has been strongly associated with the rise and fall of the conglomerate form.[77] Other labels, such as the 'chief financial officer', seem more durable. Only time will tell whether risk officers are a fad or represent a lasting organisational role, but the 'chief risk officer' (CRO) is worthy of note, being a role that surveys suggest is growing in large organisations.[78]

CROs 'represent' the risk management system but evidence varies on whether the role is responsible for the workings of this system overall, or for its design and oversight only. It is well known that officerships like this can be a dumping ground for problems, or a way of telling the world that one is serious about an issue. In this respect CROs may be an 'organisational fix', and a risky position as a potential blamee. Equally, the role may operate as a brake on excessively risk-insensitive activity.

The emergence of the CRO as a category, like that of operational and reputational risk, signifies a certain kind of transformation in status and scope of the risk management and internal control agenda. The category is the product of cultural demands for the internal allocation of responsibility. Indeed, the emphasis on the allocation of internal responsibilities for risk – 'risk ownership' – is a critical feature of imperial risk-based internal control systems.[79] The risk management of everything is characterised by an intensification of internal responsibility, accountability and 'sign off' structures, and in the private sector the CRO stands at the centre of this system.

The prevailing image of an imperial internal control system presided over by a new class of people called risk officers raises critical questions. Might the internal allocation of risk responsibility be counterproductive in any way? Do some risks slip through, or cut across, the responsibility design net? Emergent risks, which are difficult to characterise, defy easy allocation precisely because their nature and causality is poorly understood or contested. Internal accountability structures may be driven by habit and existing practice without regard for the limitations of mapping individual responsibilities to risks. Indeed, the entire process raises the spectre of a kind hyper-accountability in which the CRO acts as an internal monitor demanding 'risk auditability'.[80] Maybe CROs are just a symptom of the problem rather than its cure? They create smooth appearances of manageability and fragment and individualise risk responsibility at the organisational level. They must also spend time managing their own risk as an easy blamee.

Intelligent risk management requires that we be wary, but not entirely dismissive, of new roles with fancy titles who talk up the value-adding potential of risk management.

To the image of a risk champion with a roving role to challenge control practices must be counterpoised that of the controlling bureaucrat presiding over an unnecessarily elaborate and distracting system of internal accountability, surrounding herself with a panoply of comforting control instruments and culturally legitimate quantitative techniques.

Trust in risk numbers

The risk management of everything is closely related to an ambition to measure everything.[81] The Royal Society report in 1992 defined risk as 'the chance, in quantitative terms, of a defined hazard occurring'. Such a definition is readily familiar to a risk analysis community concerned with such diverse subjects as quality control, chemical toxicity levels and financial management. Versions of it are enshrined and institutionalised in textbooks, forging an intimate conceptual connection between risk and measurable probability. This ideal, reflecting no doubt a wider cultural 'trust in numbers',[82] is often limited in practice. It is accepted that hazards may be difficult to define and the data sets supporting probability analysis may be imperfect, but the ideal is clear.

As a statistical project with a long history one can point to an expanding frontier of formalisation in which inchoate uncertainties can become manageable risks. History shows how recalcitrant or complex interacting hazard phenomena can be broken down, new data sets can be collected for modelling and predictive purposes, and acts of God become possibilities for rational decision-making.[83] Indeed, the economist Frank Knight's famous distinction between risk and uncertainty must be taken as historical and changing rather than invariant; incalculable uncertainties can be 'tamed' as calculable risks, and the story of operational risk above reflects some of this quantitative optimism.

Measuring and modelling risk

Actuaries and financial specialists have reinvented themselves and have begun to extend the tools and techniques for market and credit risk management to operational areas, such as catastrophe and fraud risk. Quantification and measurement have become central to techniques of risk mapping and risk landscaping, which all have as their objective an overall view of the risk profile of an organisation. In short, an important sub-dimension of the risk management of everything is the expansion of the domain of rational calculation and modelling to encompass more phenomena that affect organisations.

It is widely accepted in practice that the fixation on quantification and modelling may itself be a source of risk. The CRO of Enron once wrote an article entitled 'Aiming for a single metric' and the company had a fully developed enterprise risk management system. In addition, financial risk modelling can become self-defeating when all market participants use more or less the same model. In a crisis of liquidity they will all tend to react in the same way (selling), something which collectively exacerbates the crisis.[84] Another suggestive example concerns the fact that much of the technical development in risk management has been due to corresponding advances in information and communications technology (ICT) infrastructure, advances which also create operational risks. This 'duality of risk' inherent in ICT is a metaphor for the risks of risk management more generally.[85]

Quantification and consent

Despite these difficulties, the use of quantitative techniques for risk should not be restricted when they are appropriate, but there is a need for a second-order intelligence within organisations about when this is the case.

Calculative solutions to technical problems work well in situations where there is an available database which is large, clearly defined and complete, and where a high degree of organisational and political consent about the nature of the 'risk object' exists. The science of financial risk management can make some claim to fit this idea. Where the knowledge base is less certain, risk management may have to function more as an information-gathering process, which becomes problematic as consent about the nature of the risk object diminishes.[86]

The production of consent about risk management processes demands the creation of a common language and conceptualisation of objects prior to any possible measurement activity. This consent-building process may involve non-experts and may be highly political. As the case of GM foods has shown, consent is not guaranteed. Indeed, quantification sceptics argue that complex risk management problems, such as large-scale projects involving multiple stakeholders, are essentially processes of consent management in the face of the unknowable.[87]

Intelligent risk management

Intelligent risk management practice must balance the role between calculative techniques and models, and other communicative forms, such as images and narrative (it should be borne in mind that value at risk is *both* calculative and visual). Leading organisations in the private sector will claim they do this already. Experimentation with narrative in the field of intellectual capital management is suggestive for risk management and risk mapping processes.[88] Rather than being regarded as poor quantitative tools, such maps can be effective in directing management attention and organising critical 'risk talk' within an organisation.[89] Scenario-building as pioneered by Shell in the 1970s helps to illustrate the power of softer, quantitative methods in promoting critical reflection on organisational assumptions. Intelligent risk management will embed quantitative techniques in organisational learning processes and diagnostic stories, whereby retrospective accident and error analysis can be harnessed for future planning.

Risk management and the privatisation of public life
Reputation risk and the decline of the public

The fourth and final significant risk of risk management concerns its consequences for democracy and public life. The risk management of everything implies that risk management is becoming an administrative paradigm for all forms of organisation, including government. As suggested in chapter 5, reputational risk management primarily conceptualises stakeholders as sources of threat to legitimacy, and this is the basis on which key social policy issues may be filtered and transformed by the state, by regulators and by private organisations. In this way, the rise of the risk management model and the growth of secondary risk management reflects the 'decline of the public'.[90] Key individuals and organisations with a public role seem less willing to 'risk themselves' in public. As noted already in the case of professions, a kind of social contract is being displaced by reputation risk management.

The example of the World Bank, which has recently implemented an enterprise risk management (ERM) system, illustrates that what may be at stake is often very subtle. The ERM system is concerned by definition primarily and directly with the risks to the Bank and its objectives, rather than to developing countries. Supporting such countries is part of the mission of the Bank, and a risk management system is concerned with the risks to that mission. There seems to be nothing particularly wrong with this. On the face of it, ERM is helping the Bank to focus more effectively on the first-order risks facing developing countries. And, as most business people understand very well, the best way to manage any secondary risk to reputation is to manage those first-order risks properly as part of the core business. Furthermore, we may not care what the motives of organisations like the World Bank, and their employees, really are, provided that the consequences of the work can be judged to be beneficial.

The consequences of enterprise risk management

Yet, despite this positive picture, we should be concerned. ERM contains the seeds for an essentially amoral, inward-looking and self-referential set of practices. It creates and supports a (distracting) consciousness of the organisation as being at risk in the face of the rights and claims of others. This reinforces an individualised identity for which private secondary risk management is regarded as the key to survival.

In this way, ERM creates a 'morally thin' atmosphere which

overrides any civic vitality that may have existed and which seeps into the fabric of the organisation and its participants. The latter no longer risk themselves in public and tend to engage skilfully in 'controlled self-presentation'.[91] As David Marquand has argued, 'the threats to the public domain feed on themselves' and the fact that secondary risk management has become a kind of organisational common sense is symptomatic of a society with a crisis of faith in its professions and public organisations.[92] The tight association between organisational governance and risk management reflects, rather than solves, this crisis.

Despite the critical role attributed to public communication issues in the new risk management within the public and private sectors, and the efforts to recruit publics in risk assessment processes, the public remains fundamentally externalised as problem and threat. The civic or public sphere is simply one more variable to be accommodated in standardised structures and processes of internal control.

Admittedly, reputational risk management can provide a potentially important channel between organisations and social value systems, and may in some circumstances represent a desirable social amplification of risk by forcing companies to confront social impacts. However, reputational risk management operates through, and reproduces, an essentially individualistic non-social conception of the organisation as an entity, a form of corporate personhood which, according to a 2004 documentary film entitled *The Corporation*, is psychopathic.

How can we move beyond this risk management-driven privatisation of the public sphere?

A political discourse of uncertainty

Throughout this essay, it has been hinted that an answer lies in the development of a new political discourse of uncertainty, corresponding to an experimentalism at the organisational level.[93] An earlier politics of risk was concerned to enfranchise lay views in the risk analysis and acceptance process, and to challenge the authority of experts, particularly that of scientists. The new politics of risk must retain the spirit of this critique while rehabilitating the authority of the expert. This will demand forms of leadership at the state, regulatory and corporate levels capable of developing a public language of risk that explicitly admits the possibility of failure, without this being understood as an excuse- or blame-avoiding strategy merely to manage expectations.

In the face of media and legal systems which tend to ignore 'conscientious' judgements which go wrong, this is a daunting task. A politics of uncertainty would need to develop the discursive capacity to challenge the manner in which these institutions process events. Above all this will be a public politics in which myths of perfect manageability are laid to rest but necessarily imperfect, humanly designed and operated risk management systems continue to support an engagement with unknowable futures. It will be a politics in which the essential 'as if' nature of risk management becomes the basis of public consent, rather than of an expectations gap.

8. Conclusions and suggestions

Individuals, organisations and societies have no choice but to organise in the face of uncertainty, to act 'as if' they know the risks they face. Since any form of organisation is also a form of closure, of restriction and limitation, then it is a source of risk itself. The management of uncertainty is inherently paradoxical, an effort to know the unknowable. It has been said that the present age is more aware of what it does not know, but the rise of a broad risk management mandate since the mid-1990s suggests also a continuing ambition to control and managerialise the future. This ambition is reflected in the heightened accent on internal control systems in organisations, in the creation of new risk categories and definitions to focus managerial effort, in the creation of new agents and risk responsibility structures, and in the development of new procedures and routines which seek to align risk with a moral discourse of good governance. The reach of this ambition seems to be the risk management of everything.

Risk management as a concept, though unclear, has re-entered organisational life as a demand for decisions in areas where some pretence of knowledge is a necessary defence against anxiety. The appearance of manageability is created by a material abundance of standards, textbooks and technical manuals, but the rewriting of organisational process in the name of risk is no mere technical development. It also implicates a new moral economy of organisational life at all levels: the state, public regulators, professional associations and private corporations.

In many cases, there are benefits from these developments. Not least, a better sense of risk in private and public sector organisations may enhance the quality of decisions. However, as this essay has argued, there is also a dark side to this trend, namely the emergence of secondary or reputation risk management at all levels of society.

The ubiquitous risk management blueprint is the result of a variety of factors: a response to specific scandals, opportunism by occupational communities for professional development, new modes of regulatory action and the mutation of earlier concerns with accountability. But a deeper cause is to be found at the cultural level in the rise of a distinctive individualism in which risk management services a need for protection from blame.

According to the anthropologist Mary Douglas, we choose what to fear in order to support our way of life. At present it would seem that a dominant object of fear is loss of reputation. Beneath the surface of the risk management of everything, and its claims as a value-enhancing practice, lurks a deep fear of the possible negative consequences of being responsible and answerable.

From this point of view, the risk management of everything appears like the audit of everything and its associated concerns with extending public and private accountability. The policy challenge is to avoid history repeating itself, to avoid the side effects of legitimate demands for transparency. Specifically, how can a society understand and deal with the trend whereby social agencies that have traditionally handled risk on behalf of others are becoming more preoccupied with the risks they face themselves?

The regulatory state itself is paradoxical in this respect. On the one hand, the development of specific regulatory regimes appears to be a rational response, much like auditing, to the management of first-order risks to health, financial security, etc. On the other hand, the very existence of such regulatory agencies can be interpreted as a responsibility-shifting strategy by central government concerned with its reputation.[94]

So what might be done? This essay concludes with a few suggestions.

Developing an intelligent risk management

The risks posed by the risk management of everything demand in the first instance an 'intelligent risk management' of first-order risks, and pointers have been given throughout this essay. Specifically,

1. an intelligent risk management would not allow control systems, and their advocates, to swamp managerial attention and independent critical imagination. Models and measures would be part of broader organisational narratives of uncertainty. Risk talk and 'safety imaginations'[95] will not necessarily involve the faddish risk description of everything;

2. a greater degree of disorganisation and ambiguity would be more acceptable in risk management processes than current initiatives suggest.[96] Risk management would be characterised more by learning and experiment rather than by rule-based processes. It would depend essentially on human capacities to imagine *alternative futures* to the present rather than quantitative ambitions to predict *the* future;

3. however, an intelligent risk management will not throw the baby out with the bath water; not all process and internal control is bad. To the extent that process represents the codification of accumulated wisdom, it should be sustained subject to the possibility of constant challenge. For managers, this requires an organisational capacity to question and criticise the formal risk management system itself.[97]

These suggestions are hardly original. Indeed, many organisations will claim that they are already part of their operating philosophy, that they are already intelligent. But the widespread realisation of an intelligent risk management faces many barriers. For example, the Sarbanes-Oxley legislation in the US seems to have all the characteristics likely to exacerbate a process-obsessed risk management of everything.

Limiting secondary risk management

The more challenging issue is how to contain and limit the growth of secondary risk management. Here the problem cannot be resolved at the level of the individual organisation alone. No doubt the nurturing of local cultures which are more learning-oriented and less blame-centred will help, but something more is required, namely a new political and managerial discourse of uncertainty.

The principal objective of such a discourse would be an effort to counter the individualisation processes which drive reputation risk management. For example,

1. A politics of uncertainty must explicitly acknowledge that risks are 'selected' by institutions for a mixture of cultural and economic reasons. In particular, it would need to develop public understandings and 'civic epistemologies' of how risk issues are processed and potentially amplified by the institutions of media and law.[98] In a mediatised society, not all aspects of public reactions are necessarily to be taken seriously.

    In particular, the new politics of uncertainty would demand a much clearer understanding of the basis on which public trust in organisations, including the state, is sustained or eroded.[99] It would challenge whether risk management and related disclosures by organisations really do anything to enhance public trust. Public concerns may relate more to the claimed benefits of technologies, products and services than to the effectiveness of risk and control systems.

2. The new politics of uncertainty must generate legitimacy for the possibility of failure. Indeed, in contrast to a 'spin-' or 'reputation-culture', such a political discourse would generate public trust precisely because an explicit discourse of possible failure is embedded in innovatory processes. The purpose would not be to defend individuals from blame, but to enrol the wider public in the benefits and excitement of

innovation, much as the NASA moon programme managed (temporarily) to do.

A new politics of uncertainty would not seek to assuage public anxiety and concerns with images and rhetorics of manageability and control, and would challenge assumptions that all risk is manageable. States and corporations would not need to act as if all risk is controllable and would contest media assumptions to that effect. Public understandings of expert fallibility would be a basis for trust in them rather than its opposite. Regulatory organisations would be publicly conceived of more as laboratories rather than as insurers. For governments and regulators, the test of good governance would not necessarily be the speed of their reaction to failure; on the contrary, it might be their ability, in Peter Senge's phrase, 'to take two aspirin and wait'.

Only time will tell, but both the measured response in the *Every Child Matters* green paper following a series of high-profile failures in child protection, and the FSA and HM Treasury's response to the Penrose Inquiry into the Equitable Life collapse, could turn out to be important turning points in the state's capacity to withstand pressure for knee-jerk reactions to crisis.

3. Crucially, a new politics of uncertainty must provide the necessary, if not sufficient, institutional conditions, for intelligent trust in expert judgement to flourish, and for the recovery and development of the idea of honest professional opinion. We need to imagine and create 'safe havens' for professional and expert judgement. These havens would be safe in the sense of providing a space for decision-making where competence may flourish and express itself. While such safe havens would not be a return to unaccountable expertise, the challenge posed by an earlier politics of uncertainty, experts could be assured of a proportionality of response to decisions which turn out in retrospect to have been wrong, though honestly and reasonably made.

Safe havens would, of course, require real institutional innovation. These might include experimentation with no fault insurance mechanisms, as proposed by the Chief Medical Officer last year for clinical negligence, on the basis that they are much more conducive to the honest acceptance and explanation of failure, and therefore permit greater learning, than liability law. Another model, this time from the academy, is that of tenure. It would be interesting to revisit the potential for tenure mechanisms in other professions as a basis for the security of expert judgement. Finally there is almost certainly a role for professional bodies and associations in identifying and regulating these safe havens, and creating forms of peer review that help ensure they are not exploited by unscrupulous practitioners. Although these changes might seem peripheral, as the risk management of everything has shown, we should not underestimate the power of specific innovations to spread and become a template that permeates a much wider set of institutional cultures.

4. A new politics of uncertainty will challenge the 'small print' or disclaimer society that we have become in the interests of making secondary risk management strategies publicly visible and contestable. *When disclaimer paragraphs are longer than the professional opinions they follow, we know something has gone wrong.* In the interests of transparency, small print should be made large and ruled out as a secondary risk management ploy.

5. Given the significance of large organisations in economic and public life, the elements of a new politics of uncertainty could be assembled at this level of society and filter 'upwards' into the political domain, just as other ideas have done. A possible launch pad might be the public mission of regulatory organisations, positioned as they are between political processes and the wider environment of public and private organisations. There are some signs of this in the risk-based self-description of some agencies, but these organisations are

themselves constantly vulnerable to 'political risk'. Governments and opposition have a responsibility to uphold their side of the bargain that has seen complex and risky decisions delegated to independent regulators, and not make hay every time something goes awry.

These are just a few speculative and necessarily incomplete suggestions but they frame the challenge posed by the risks of the risk management of everything. The risk management of everything, and the specific growth of secondary risk management, has a dark side which is threatening the state, regulatory bodies, corporations and the individual experts on which so many individuals in society rely. If we must act as if we know the risks we face, then we must also create forms of risk management, and a related politics of uncertainty, which allows us to do this in more, rather than less, intelligent ways.

Notes

1   See M Douglas and A Wildavsky, *Risk and Culture* (Berkeley: University of California Press, 1983): 1.

2   For a flavour of this broad agenda see EBR, *Managing Risk* (London: European Business Forum in association with Marsh, 2003); 'Living Dangerously', *Economist Survey*, January 2004.

3   See for example, National Audit Office, *Supporting Innovation: managing risk in government departments* (London: National Audit Office, 2000); Health and Safety Executive, *Reducing Risk, Protecting People: HSE's decision-making process* (London: HSE, 2001); Cabinet Office Strategy Unit, *Risk: improving government's capability to handle risk and uncertainty* (London: Cabinet Office, 2002); S Dibb, *Winning the Risk Game* (London: National Consumer Council, 2003); C Raban and E Turner, *Academic Risk: quality risk management in higher education* (London: Higher Education Funding Council, 2003).

4   ICAEW, *Internal Control: guidance for the directors of listed companies incorporated in the United Kingdom*, (London: Institute of Chartered Accountants in England and Wales, 1999).

5   See for example, M Hanley, *Integrated Risk Management* (London: FT books, 1999); Economist Intelligence Unit, *Enterprise Risk Management – implementing new solutions* (London: Economist, 2001); J Larkin, *Strategic Reputation Risk Management* (London: Palgrave Macmillan, 2002); J Lam, *Enterprise Risk Management – from incentives to controls* (London: John Wiley, 2003).

6   The UK Treasury website has links to a number of these associations as knowledge resources, including the Institute of Internal Auditors, the Global Association of Risk Professionals, the Institute of Risk Management.

7   See for example, PwC/IFAC, *Enhancing Shareholder Wealth by Better Managing Business Risk* (New York: PricewaterhouseCoopers/International Federation of Accountants, 1999).

8   See B Flyvbjerg, N Bruzelius and W Rothengatter, *Megaprojects and Risk: an anatomy of ambition* (Cambridge: Cambridge University Press, 2003).

9   See B Hunt, *The Timid Corporation: why business is terrified of taking risk* (London: John Wiley, 2003), chapter 3.

10   See B Fischoff, SR Watson and C Hope, 'Defining Risk', *Policy Sciences* 17 (1984): 123–39.

11   E Rosa, 'Meta-theoretical foundations for post-normal risk', *Journal of Risk Research* 1 (1998): 15–44.

12   See U Beck, *Risk Society – towards a new modernity* (London: Sage, 1992).

13   See P Bernstein, *Against the Gods: the remarkable story of risk* (New York: John Wiley and Sons, 1996).

14   The idea, used throughout this essay, of 'intelligent' risk management is borrowed from O O'Neill, 'Intelligent trust, intelligent accountability', paper presented at the CBR/CARR workshop on *Soft Risks, Hard Lessons: using corporate governance to manage legal, ethical and reputational uncertainties*, (Cambridge: Cambridge University, January 2004).

15   See C Hood, H Rothstein and R Baldwin, *The Government of Risk* (Oxford: Oxford University Press, 2001).

16   See the preface to C Hood and D Jones (eds), *Accident and Design: contemporary debates in risk management* (London: UCL Press, 1996).

17   See National Research Council, *Understanding Risk: informing decisions in a democratic society* (Washington DC: National Academy Press, 1996); for further discussion see also D Okrent and NF Pidgeon (eds), 'Risk assessment versus risk perception'. Special volume of *Reliability Engineering and System Safety* 59 (1998): 1–159.

18   See Cabinet Office Strategy Unit, *Risk: improving government's capability to handle risk and uncertainty* (London: Cabinet Office, 2002), 16.

19   See the UK Treasury risk support homepage; available at www.hm-treasury. gov.uk/documents/public_spending_and_services/risk/pss_risk_index.cfm.

20   Phrase attributed to G Mulgan speaking at a conference entitled 'Panic Attack', London: The Royal Institution, 9 May 2003.

21   See H Rothstein, 'Precautionary bans or sacrificial lambs? Participative risk regulation and the reform of the UK food safety regime', *Public Administration* (forthcoming, 2004).

22   See B Hutter, *Risk and Regulation* (Oxford: Oxford University Press, 2000).

23   See C Sunstein, 'The laws of fear', *Harvard Law Review* 115 (2002): 1119–68.

24   See for example, A Stirling, 'Risk at a turning point?', *Journal of Risk Research* 1 (1998): 97–109; See also D Okrent and NF Pidgeon, 'Risk assessment versus risk perception'.

25   Based on an allegedly leaked memorandum reported in the UK press in late April 2004.

26   See C Hood, 'The risk game and the blame game', *Government and Opposition* 37 (2002): 15–37.

27   See P Skidmore, P Miller and J Chapman, *The Long Game: how regulators and companies can both win* (London: Demos, 2003).

28   See I Ayres and J Braithwaite, *Responsive Regulation: transcending the deregulation debate* (New York: Oxford University Press, 1992).

29   This is perhaps most explicit in the case of the UK Financial Services Authority. See FSA, *A New Regulator for the New Millennium* (London: Financial Services Authority, January 2000); J Black, 'Mapping the contours of contemporary financial services regulation', CARR Discussion Paper 17 (London: London School of Economics, 2003); see also the Audit Commission, *Strategic Regulation: minimizing the burden, maximizing the impact* (London: Audit Commission, 2003).

30   DTI Innovation Report, *Competing in the Global Economy: the innovation challenge* (London: DTI, 2003); FSA, *A New Regulator for the New Millennium.*

31   See K Walshe and T Sheldon, 'Dealing with clinical risk: implications of the rise of evidence-based health care', *Public Money and Management,* October–December (1998): 15–20.

32   See P Day and R Klein, *The NHS Improvers: a study of the commission for health improvement* (London: King's Fund, 2004).

33   Nowhere is this more evident than in the requirements of the US Sarbanes-Oxley Act, section 404, which is likely to become a global blueprint.

34   See J Freedman, 'Accountants and corporate governance: filling a legal vacuum', *Political Quarterly* 64 (1993): 285–97.

35   OECD, *Principles of Corporate Governance* (Paris: OECD, 1998).

36   See COSO, *Internal Control: integrated framework* (Committee of Sponsoring Organizations of the Treadway Commission, 1991); available at www.coso.org/publications.htm.

37   See the ISO 9000 series of standards published by the International Standards Organization, based on an earlier standard, BS5075, issued by the British Standards Institute; See J Tate, 'National varieties of standardization' in D Sokice and P Hall (eds), *Varieties of Capitalism* (New York: Oxford University Press, 2001): 442–73.

38   See AS/NZS, *Risk Management* (Sydney and Wellington: Standards Australia and Standards New Zealand, 1995); CSA, *CAN/CSA – Q850–97, Risk Management Guidelines for Decision Makers, a national standard for Canada.* (Canadian Standards Association, 1997); BSI, *BSI 6079-3. Project Management – Part 3: guide to the management of business-related project risk* (London: British Standards Institute, 1999); JIS, *JIS Q 2001, Guidelines for the Development and Implementation of Risk Management System* (Tokyo: Japanese Standards Association, 2001).

39   See COSO, *Enterprise Risk Management Framework: exposure draft* (Committee of the Sponsoring Organizations of the Treadway Commission, 2003); available at www.coso.org/publications.htm.

40   See 'Meet the Riskmongers', *The Economist,* 18 July 1998: 93–4.

41   See BA Turner and N Pidgeon, *Man-Made Disasters,* 2nd edn (Oxford: Butterworth-Heinemann, 1997): pp 185–6.

42   See C Swinson, 'Limitations of fail-safe systems', *Accountancy,* May (2004): 26.

43   This section is based on M Power, 'The invention of operational risk', *International Review of Political Economy* (forthcoming).

44 See Group of Thirty, *Derivatives: practices and principles* (Washington, DC: Group of Thirty, 1993).

45 See Basel Committee on Banking Supervision, *Sound Practices for the Management and Supervision of Operational Risk* (Basel: Bank for International Settlements, December 2001).

46 'Boundary objects are those objects that both inhabit several communities of practice and satisfy the informational requirements of each of them. Boundary objects are thus both plastic enough to adapt to local needs and constraints of the several parties employing them, yet robust enough to maintain common identity across sites. They are weakly structured in common use and become strongly structured in individual site use.' G Bowker and S Star, *Sorting Things Out: classification and its consequences* (Cambridge, MA: The MIT Press, 2000), p 297.

47 See C Fombrun and V Rindova, 'The road to transparency: reputation management at Royal Dutch Shell 1977–96' in M Schultz, MJ Hatch and HL Larsen (eds), *The Expressive Organization: linking identity, reputation and the corporate brand* (Oxford: Oxford University Press, 2000), pp 77–96.

48 R Lofstedt and O Renn, 'The Brent Spar controversy: an example of risk communication gone wrong', *Risk Analysis* 17, no 2 (1997): 131–6.

49 See the essays in NF Pidgeon, RK Kasperson and P Slovic (eds), *The Social Amplification of Risk* (Cambridge: Cambridge University Press, 2003).

50 For example see *Reputation and the Bottom Line: a communications guide to reporting on corporate reputation* (London: Institute of Public Relations, MORI and Business in the Community, 2003).

51 See 'Barclays banks on a good name', *Financial Times*, 19 Feb 2004.

52 See M Power, 'Risk management and the responsible organization' in R Ericson and A Doyle (eds), *Risk and Morality* (Toronto: University of Toronto Press, 2003).

53 B Hunt, 'Corporate social responsibility as a new self-regulation', paper presented at the Centre for Analysis of Risk and Regulation, London School of Economics, April 2004; see also B Hunt, 'Concerned companies', *Spiked-Risk,* 14 April 2004, available at: www.spiked-online.com.

54 A Giddens, *Runaway World: how globalization is reshaping our lives* (London: Routledge, 2003).

55 NF Pidgeon, RK Kasperson and P Slovic (eds), *The Social Amplification of Risk*.

56 See N Luhmann, *Risk: a sociological theory* (Berlin: de Gruyter, 1992).

57 See E Abrahamson, 'Managerial fads and fashions: the diffusion and rejection of innovations', *Academy of Management Review* 16 (1991): 586–612.

58 See L Edelman, SR Fuller and I Mara-Drita, 'Diversity rhetoric and the managerialization of law', *American Journal of Sociology* 106 (2001): 1596.

59 For example, G Hamel and L Valikangas, 'The quest for resilience', *Harvard Business Review,* September (2003).

60 M Power, *The Audit Explosion* (London: Demos, 1994).

61 Group of Thirty, *Derivatives: practices and principles.*

62   See M Power, *The Audit Implosion: managing risk from the inside* (London: ICAEW, 1999).

63   See M Douglas and A Wildavsky, *Risk and Culture*, p 21.

64   BA Turner and N Pidgeon, *Man-Made Disasters*. This is also called 'disaster incubation theory'. See the review essay by J Rijpma, 'From deadlock to dead-end: the normal accidents – high reliability debate revisited', *Journal of Contingencies and Crisis Management* 11, no 1 (2003): 37–45.

65   D Vaughan, *The Challenger Launch Decision* (Chicago: University of Chicago Press, 1996).

66   See B Hunt, *The Timid Corporation*.

67   See C Hood, 'The risk game and the blame game'.

68   'Money laundering tip-offs set to double', *Financial Times*, 1 March 2004.

69   See L Edelman et al, 'Diversity rhetoric and the managerialization of law'.

70   See SB Sitkin and RJ Bies, 'The legalization of organizations: a multi-theoretical perspective' in SB Sitkin and RJ Bies (eds), *The Legalistic Organization* (Thousand Oaks, CA: Sage, 1994) pp 19–49.

71   F Furedi, *The Culture of Fear: risk-taking and the morality of low expectations* (London and New York: Continuum International, 1997).

72   See P Bernstein, 'The new religion of risk management', *Harvard Business Review*, March/April (1996): 47–51.

73   See L Clarke, *Mission Improbable: using fantasy documents to tame disaster* (Chicago: University of Chicago Press, 1999).

74   See R Holt, 'Risk management: the talking cure', *Organization* 11 (2004): 261.

75   This section is based mainly on M Power, 'The rise of the chief risk officer', in B Hutter and M Power (eds), *Organizational Encounters with Risk* (Cambridge: Cambridge University Press, forthcoming).

76   D Gray, 'Wanted: Chief Ignorance Officer', *Harvard Business Review,* November (2003): 22–4.

77   F Dobbin, J Dierkes, M-S Kwok and D Zorn, 'The rise and stagnation of the COO: fad and fashion in corporate titles', discussion paper (Princeton, NJ: Department of Sociology, Princeton University, 2001); available at www.wjh.harvard.edu/~dobbin/COOpaper.doc

78   J Miccolis, K Hively and B Merkley, *Enterprise Risk Management: trends and emerging practices* (Altamonte Springs, FL: The Institute of Internal Auditors Research Foundation, 2001).

79   M Douglas, 'Les Risques du Fonctionnaire du Risque: La Diversité des Institutions et la Répartition des Risques' (The Risks of the Risk Officer: Diversity of Institutions and The Distribution of Risks), *La Revue Alliage* 40 (2002): 61–74; available at www.tribunes.com/tribune/alliage/40/douglas_40.htm.

80   See M Power, *The Audit Society: rituals of verification* (Oxford: Oxford University Press, 1997).

81   See M Power, 'Counting, control and calculation: reflections on measuring and managing', *Human Relations* 57, no 6 (2004).

82   T Porter, *Trust in Numbers* (Princeton: Princeton University Press, 1995).

83   P Bernstein, *Against the Gods: the remarkable story of risk*; and P Bernstein, 'The new religion of risk management'.

84   J Daniellson, 'VaR: a castle built on sand', *The Financial Regulator* 5, no 2 (2001): 46–50.

85   See C Ciborra, ' The duality of risk', CARR Discussion Paper (London: London School of Economics, forthcoming 2004).

86   See M Douglas and A Wildavsky, *Risk and Culture*; see also S Hilgartner, 'The social construction of risk objects: or, how to pry open networks of risk', in J Short and L Clarke (eds), *Organizations, Uncertainties and Risks* (Boulder: Westview Press, 1992), pp 39–53.

87   See B Flyvbjerg et al, *Megaprojects and Risk*.

88   J Mouritsen, 'Intellectual capital and the "capable firm": narrating, visualising and numbering for managing knowledge', *Accounting, Organizations and Society* 26 (2001): 735–62.

89   R Simon, 'How risky is your company?' *Harvard Business Review* 77, May/June (1999): 85–94.

90   See D Marquand, *The Decline of the Public* (Cambridge: Polity Press, 2004).

91   See R Williams, *Lost Icons: reflections on cultural bereavement* (London: Continuum, 2000).

92   See D Marquand, *The Decline of the Public*, p 132.

93   See U Beck, 'Risk and power: why we need a "culture of uncertainty" in EBR', *Managing Risk*, pp 22–6.

94   See C Hood, 'The risk game and the blame game'.

95   N Pidgeon and M O'Leary, 'Man-made disasters: why technology and organizations (sometimes) fail', *Safety Science* 34 (2000): 15–30.

96   See R Holt, 'Risk management: the talking cure'.

97   Ibid.

98   The concept of 'civil epistemology' has been developed by Sheila Jasanoff.

99   See 'Media blamed for loss of trust in government', *Guardian*, Thursday 6 May 2004.

DEMOS – Licence to Publish

THE WORK (AS DEFINED BELOW) IS PROVIDED UNDER THE TERMS OF THIS LICENCE ("LICENCE"). THE WORK IS PROTECTED BY COPYRIGHT AND/OR OTHER APPLICABLE LAW. ANY USE OF THE WORK OTHER THAN AS AUTHORIZED UNDER THIS LICENCE IS PROHIBITED. BY EXERCISING ANY RIGHTS TO THE WORK PROVIDED HERE, YOU ACCEPT AND AGREE TO BE BOUND BY THE TERMS OF THIS LICENCE. DEMOS GRANTS YOU THE RIGHTS CONTAINED HERE IN CONSIDERATION OF YOUR ACCEPTANCE OF SUCH TERMS AND CONDITIONS.

1. **Definitions**
   a   **"Collective Work"** means a work, such as a periodical issue, anthology or encyclopedia, in which the Work in its entirety in unmodified form, along with a number of other contributions, constituting separate and independent works in themselves, are assembled into a collective whole. A work that constitutes a Collective Work will not be considered a Derivative Work (as defined below) for the purposes of this Licence.
   b   **"Derivative Work"** means a work based upon the Work or upon the Work and other pre-existing works, such as a musical arrangement, dramatization, fictionalization, motion picture version, sound recording, art reproduction, abridgment, condensation, or any other form in which the Work may be recast, transformed, or adapted, except that a work that constitutes a Collective Work or a translation from English into another language will not be considered a Derivative Work for the purpose of this Licence.
   c   **"Licensor"** means the individual or entity that offers the Work under the terms of this Licence.
   d   **"Original Author"** means the individual or entity who created the Work.
   e   **"Work"** means the copyrightable work of authorship offered under the terms of this Licence.
   f   **"You"** means an individual or entity exercising rights under this Licence who has not previously violated the terms of this Licence with respect to the Work, or who has received express permission from DEMOS to exercise rights under this Licence despite a previous violation.
2. **Fair Use Rights.** Nothing in this licence is intended to reduce, limit, or restrict any rights arising from fair use, first sale or other limitations on the exclusive rights of the copyright owner under copyright law or other applicable laws.
3. **Licence Grant.** Subject to the terms and conditions of this Licence, Licensor hereby grants You a worldwide, royalty-free, non-exclusive, perpetual (for the duration of the applicable copyright) licence to exercise the rights in the Work as stated below:
   a   to reproduce the Work, to incorporate the Work into one or more Collective Works, and to reproduce the Work as incorporated in the Collective Works;
   b   to distribute copies or phonorecords of, display publicly, perform publicly, and perform publicly by means of a digital audio transmission the Work including as incorporated in Collective Works;
   The above rights may be exercised in all media and formats whether now known or hereafter devised. The above rights include the right to make such modifications as are technically necessary to exercise the rights in other media and formats. All rights not expressly granted by Licensor are hereby reserved.
4. **Restrictions.** The licence granted in Section 3 above is expressly made subject to and limited by the following restrictions:
   a   You may distribute, publicly display, publicly perform, or publicly digitally perform the Work only under the terms of this Licence, and You must include a copy of, or the Uniform Resource Identifier for, this Licence with every copy or phonorecord of the Work You distribute, publicly display, publicly perform, or publicly digitally perform. You may not offer or impose any terms on the Work that alter or restrict the terms of this Licence or the recipients' exercise of the rights granted hereunder. You may not sublicence the Work. You must keep intact all notices that refer to this Licence and to the disclaimer of warranties. You may not distribute, publicly display, publicly perform, or publicly digitally perform the Work with any technological measures that control access or use of the Work in a manner inconsistent with the terms of this Licence Agreement. The above applies to the Work as incorporated in a Collective Work, but this does not require the Collective Work apart from the Work itself to be made subject to the terms of this Licence. If You create a Collective Work, upon notice from any Licencor You must, to the extent practicable, remove from the Collective Work any reference to such Licensor or the Original Author, as requested.
   b   You may not exercise any of the rights granted to You in Section 3 above in any manner that is primarily intended for or directed toward commercial advantage or private monetary

compensation. The exchange of the Work for other copyrighted works by means of digital file-sharing or otherwise shall not be considered to be intended for or directed toward commercial advantage or private monetary compensation, provided there is no payment of any monetary compensation in connection with the exchange of copyrighted works.

   c If you distribute, publicly display, publicly perform, or publicly digitally perform the Work or any Collective Works, You must keep intact all copyright notices for the Work and give the Original Author credit reasonable to the medium or means You are utilizing by conveying the name (or pseudonym if applicable) of the Original Author if supplied; the title of the Work if supplied. Such credit may be implemented in any reasonable manner; provided, however, that in the case of a Collective Work, at a minimum such credit will appear where any other comparable authorship credit appears and in a manner at least as prominent as such other comparable authorship credit.

5. Representations, Warranties and Disclaimer

   a By offering the Work for public release under this Licence, Licensor represents and warrants that, to the best of Licensor's knowledge after reasonable inquiry:

      i Licensor has secured all rights in the Work necessary to grant the licence rights hereunder and to permit the lawful exercise of the rights granted hereunder without You having any obligation to pay any royalties, compulsory licence fees, residuals or any other payments;

      ii The Work does not infringe the copyright, trademark, publicity rights, common law rights or any other right of any third party or constitute defamation, invasion of privacy or other tortious injury to any third party.

   b EXCEPT AS EXPRESSLY STATED IN THIS LICENCE OR OTHERWISE AGREED IN WRITING OR REQUIRED BY APPLICABLE LAW, THE WORK IS LICENCED ON AN "AS IS" BASIS, WITHOUT WARRANTIES OF ANY KIND, EITHER EXPRESS OR IMPLIED INCLUDING, WITHOUT LIMITATION, ANY WARRANTIES REGARDING THE CONTENTS OR ACCURACY OF THE WORK.

6. Limitation on Liability. EXCEPT TO THE EXTENT REQUIRED BY APPLICABLE LAW, AND EXCEPT FOR DAMAGES ARISING FROM LIABILITY TO A THIRD PARTY RESULTING FROM BREACH OF THE WARRANTIES IN SECTION 5, IN NO EVENT WILL LICENSOR BE LIABLE TO YOU ON ANY LEGAL THEORY FOR ANY SPECIAL, INCIDENTAL, CONSEQUENTIAL, PUNITIVE OR EXEMPLARY DAMAGES ARISING OUT OF THIS LICENCE OR THE USE OF THE WORK, EVEN IF LICENSOR HAS BEEN ADVISED OF THE POSSIBILITY OF SUCH DAMAGES.

7. Termination

   a This Licence and the rights granted hereunder will terminate automatically upon any breach by You of the terms of this Licence. Individuals or entities who have received Collective Works from You under this Licence, however, will not have their licences terminated provided such individuals or entities remain in full compliance with those licences. Sections 1, 2, 5, 6, 7, and 8 will survive any termination of this Licence.

   b Subject to the above terms and conditions, the licence granted here is perpetual (for the duration of the applicable copyright in the Work). Notwithstanding the above, Licensor reserves the right to release the Work under different licence terms or to stop distributing the Work at any time; provided, however that any such election will not serve to withdraw this Licence (or any other licence that has been, or is required to be, granted under the terms of this Licence), and this Licence will continue in full force and effect unless terminated as stated above.

8. Miscellaneous

   a Each time You distribute or publicly digitally perform the Work or a Collective Work, DEMOS offers to the recipient a licence to the Work on the same terms and conditions as the licence granted to You under this Licence.

   b If any provision of this Licence is invalid or unenforceable under applicable law, it shall not affect the validity or enforceability of the remainder of the terms of this Licence, and without further action by the parties to this agreement, such provision shall be reformed to the minimum extent necessary to make such provision valid and enforceable.

   c No term or provision of this Licence shall be deemed waived and no breach consented to unless such waiver or consent shall be in writing and signed by the party to be charged with such waiver or consent.

   d This Licence constitutes the entire agreement between the parties with respect to the Work licensed here. There are no understandings, agreements or representations with respect to the Work not specified here. Licensor shall not be bound by any additional provisions that may appear in any communication from You. This Licence may not be modified without the mutual written agreement of DEMOS and You.